LISTEN UP!

THE POWER OF PRESENCE: LISTENING SKILLS FOR EXCEPTIONAL SALES PERFORMANCE

DR. MOE TAREK EL KASSAR

Made with ♥ on the Notion Press Platform
www.notionpress.com

This book is dedicated to all the salespeople who strive to not just hear but truly listen to their clients. May the insights and strategies shared within these pages empower you to build stronger relationships, close more deals, and ultimately, make a greater impact on the world of sales.

Contents

Foreword

In today's fast-paced world, it's easy to become so focused on the next sale, the next meeting, or the next goal that we forget the power of truly listening to those around us. Whether it's our clients, colleagues, or loved ones, active listening is the key to building stronger relationships, understanding others' needs, and ultimately, achieving success.

With 'Listen Up', you'll discover the essential techniques and strategies for listening skills in the world of sales. From understanding the psychology behind communication to mastering the techniques of active listening, this book is packed with practical tips and real-life examples to help you improve your listening skills and take your sales game to the next level.

So whether you're just starting out in sales or are a seasoned pro, turn the page and begin your journey towards becoming a master listener. The world of sales - and beyond - is waiting for you.

Preface

In this book, we will explore the art and science of active listening, and how it can be applied in the world of sales. We will delve into the psychology of communication and the barriers that can prevent us from truly hearing what others have to say. We will also explore the different types of listening, and how to use effective questioning techniques to gain a deeper understanding of our client's needs.

Through real-life examples and practical exercises, we will learn how to apply active listening in different sales scenarios, from virtual meetings to in-person negotiations. We will also explore how to use nonverbal cues to better understand our client's emotions and thoughts, and how to use active listening to build trust and rapport, negotiate and close more deals.

This book is not only for salespeople, but for anyone who wants to improve their listening skills, build stronger relationships, and achieve success in their personal and professional life.

I hope that the insights and strategies shared in this book will empower you to become a master listener, and to make a greater impact on the world of sales and beyond.

Acknowledgements

Writing this book would not have been possible without the support and guidance of many individuals. I would like to express my deepest gratitude to:

- My family, for their unwavering support and encouragement throughout this journey.
- The experts in the field of communication, psychology and sales, whose research and insights I have referenced and whose knowledge has been fundamental for the creation of this book.
- My colleagues, for sharing their personal experiences, and for providing case studies that helped to illustrate the concepts discussed in this book.
- All the readers and reviewers, who provided valuable feedback, and helped me to improve the quality of this book.

Finally, I would like to thank you, the reader, for taking the time to read this book and for your interest in improving your listening skills. I hope that this book will be of great value to you, and that it will help you to build stronger relationships, close more deals and achieve success in your personal and professional life.

Prologue

As a salesperson, the ability to truly listen to your clients is essential for building strong relationships, understanding their needs, and ultimately closing more deals. But in today's fast-paced world, where technology and distractions are constantly vying for our attention, it can be easy to fall into the trap of simply "hearing" rather than truly listening.

That's where this book comes in. In the pages that follow, we'll explore the art and science of active listening, and how it can be applied to the world of sales. From understanding the psychology behind communication, to mastering the techniques of active listening, this book is packed with practical tips and real-life examples to help you improve your listening skills and take your sales game to the next level.

So whether you're just starting out in sales or are a seasoned pro, turn the page and begin your journey towards becoming a master listener. The world of sales- and beyond- is waiting for you.

CHAPTER ONE

Introduction: The importance of listening skills in sales performance

Listening skills are crucial for salespeople because they are the foundation for effective communication and building relationships with customers. Good listening skills allow salespeople to truly understand their customers' needs, wants, and concerns, which in turn helps them to provide personalized and effective solutions.

There are several key benefits to having strong listening skills in sales, including:

Building trust and rapport: Good listeners are able to build trust and rapport with their customers, which is essential for building long-term relationships. By showing that you are truly interested in what the customer has to say, you can create a sense of connection and establish trust.

Identifying customer needs: Effective listening allows salespeople to identify their customers' needs, wants, and concerns, which is crucial for providing personalized solutions. A salesperson that can listen carefully to the customer and ask the right questions can better understand the customer's needs and can present solutions that match the customer's requirements.

Handling objections: Good listening skills also help salespeople to identify and handle objections effectively. By listening carefully to the customer's concerns and objections, salespeople can address them directly and find ways to overcome them.

Improving communication: Listening skills are also important for effective communication in sales. By listening carefully to the customer, salespeople can ensure that they are providing accurate and relevant information, which in turn increases the chances of closing a sale.

Improving customer satisfaction: Good listening skills can also help to improve customer satisfaction by ensuring that the customer's needs are being met. When a customer feels that their needs have been understood and addressed, they are more likely to be satisfied with the service and the product.

In summary, listening skills are essential for salespeople because they are the foundation for effective communication, building trust and rapport with customers, identifying customer needs and handling objections effectively. It also helps in improving communication and customer satisfaction which ultimately leads to more sales.

CHAPTER TWO

The Basics of Listening in Sales

Listening in a sales context

Listening in a sales context refers to the act of paying attention and interpreting verbal and nonverbal communication from customers in order to understand their needs, wants, and concerns. This can include actively listening to what the customer is saying, interpreting nonverbal cues such as body language, and asking open-ended questions to gain a deeper understanding of the customer's perspective.

In a sales context, listening involves more than just hearing the customer's words, it requires the salesperson to actively process and comprehend the information, to interpret the customer's verbal and nonverbal message and to respond appropriately. Listening actively also means that the salesperson should be able to identify the customer's needs, wants, and concerns, as well as buying signals, and objections.

Effective listening in a sales context helps to build trust and rapport with the customer, to identify the customer's needs and wants, to handle objections effectively, and to improve communication and customer satisfaction. This can lead to a more successful sales outcome, as the salesperson is better able to provide personalized solutions that meet the customer's specific needs.

There are a few key aspects of listening in a sales context that are important to understand:

Active listening: This involves actively focusing on what the customer is saying and responding in a way that shows you are engaged and interested in their needs. Active listening can include techniques such as paraphrasing, reflecting, and summarizing, which demonstrate to the customer that you are paying attention and understanding their perspective.

Empathetic listening: This type of listening is about understanding the customer's emotional state and feeling their perspective. This can help to build trust and rapport with the customer, as they feel heard and understood.

Critical listening: This type of listening is about evaluating the information that is being presented and asking follow-up questions to gain a deeper understanding of the customer's needs and to identify any potential objections.

Reflective listening: This type of listening is about focusing on the customer's needs and feelings, reflecting back on what the customer is saying, and trying to understand their perspective. This can be useful in handling objections and resolving conflicts.

Summarizing: This type of listening is about focusing on the key points discussed during the conversation and putting them in a nutshell, this can help the salesperson to understand the customer's needs and wants and to ensure that everyone is on the same page.

It's important to note that listening in a sales context is not a one-time event, it's an ongoing process that requires attention and focus throughout the interaction with the customer. Salespeople should be able to listen actively, critically, empathically, reflectively, and summarize to be able to understand the customer's needs, wants, and concerns, and to provide personalized solutions.

Also, it's important to note that listening skills are not only important for salespeople but for anyone working in a customer service or communication-related job. Listening effectively is crucial to understanding the customer's needs and providing a high-quality service.

Active listening

Active listening is a type of listening that involves paying close attention to what the customer is saying, both verbally and nonverbally. It requires the salesperson to focus on the customer's words, tone of voice, and body language in order to fully understand their message. Active listening also involves using techniques such as paraphrasing and reflecting to show the customer that their words and ideas are being heard and understood.

Active listening is particularly important in a sales context because it allows the salesperson to understand the customer's needs and concerns in depth. This, in turn, allows the salesperson to provide personalized solutions that match the customer's specific needs. Additionally, active listening helps to build trust and rapport with the customer, as it demonstrates that the salesperson is truly interested in what the customer has to say.

Active listening also includes paying attention to verbal and nonverbal cues and buying signals which is important in identifying the customer's buying intention. It also allows the salesperson to identify and handle objections effectively by addressing them directly and finding ways to overcome them.

In summary, active listening is a vital skill for salespeople, as it helps them to understand their customers' needs, build trust and rapport, and provide personalized solutions that meet the customer's specific needs. It also helps to identify buying signals and handle objections effectively, which can increase the chances of closing a sale.

Here is an example of active listening in a sales context:

A customer walks into a car dealership and tells the salesperson that they are looking for a new car to replace their current one, which is getting old and unreliable. The salesperson actively listens to the customer by paying attention to their words, tone of voice, and body language. They ask open-ended questions such as "What type of car are you looking for?" and "What features are most important to you?" They also paraphrase what the customer is saying, such as "So you're looking for a car that is more reliable and has more modern features than your current one?"

By actively listening and engaging with the customer, the salesperson is able to gain a deeper understanding of the customer's needs and can recommend specific cars that match the customer's criteria.

In this example, the salesperson has demonstrated active listening by paying close attention to the customer, asking questions to gain a deeper understanding, and paraphrasing the customer's words to ensure that they have fully understood their needs. By doing so, the salesperson is able to provide a personalized solution that matches the customer's specific needs and increase the chances of closing a sale.

Active listening is an important skill that can be applied in various scenarios, not only in sales but also in other contexts such as customer service, management, and personal relationships.

Here is a second example of active listening in a sales context:

A customer contacts a salesperson at a technology company to inquire about a new software program. The customer expresses concerns about the cost and mentions that they have a limited budget. The salesperson actively listens to the customer by paying attention to their words, tone of voice, and body language. They ask open-ended questions such as "What is your budget for this software?" and "What features are most important to you?" They also paraphrase what the customer is saying, such as "So cost is a concern for you and you have a budget in mind?"

By actively listening and engaging with the customer, the salesperson is able to understand the customer's budget constraints and can recommend a software package that fits within their budget while still meeting their needs. The salesperson also offers a payment plan that aligns with the customer's budget. The customer feels that their needs were heard and understood and is more likely to make a purchase.

In this example, the salesperson has demonstrated active listening by paying close attention to the customer, asking questions to gain a deeper understanding, and paraphrasing the customer's words to ensure that they have fully understood their needs and concerns.

By doing so, the salesperson is able to provide a personalized solution that matches the customer's specific needs and budget, addressing their concerns and increasing the chances of closing a sale.

Here is a third example of active listening in a sales context:

A customer calls into a travel agency and expresses an interest in planning a vacation to a specific destination. The salesperson actively listens to the customer by paying attention to their words, tone of voice, and asking open-ended questions to understand what the customer is looking for. The customer mentions that they are looking for a relaxing vacation and that they are interested in visiting the beach and the spa. The salesperson confirms the customer's interest by paraphrasing what the customer is saying and then providing recommendations for destinations that offer both beach and spa amenities. The salesperson also asks about the customer's budget and travel dates to ensure that the recommendations align with the customer's needs and preferences.

By actively listening and engaging with the customer, the salesperson is able to understand the customer's specific needs and wants, and can provide personalized recommendations that align with the customer's preferences. This makes the customer feel heard and understood, increases the chances of closing a sale and improves the customer satisfaction.

In this example, the salesperson has demonstrated active listening by paying close attention to the customer, asking questions to gain a deeper understanding, and paraphrasing the customer's words to ensure that they have fully understood their needs and preferences. By doing so, the salesperson is able to provide a personalized solution that matches the customer's specific needs, preferences, and budget which increases the chances of closing a sale.

Empathetic listening

Empathetic listening is a specific type of active listening that involves not only understanding the words that a person is saying, but also understanding their emotions and perspective. It requires the listener to put themselves in the speaker's shoes and to try to understand their feelings and experiences.

Empathetic listening is particularly important in a sales context because it allows the salesperson to understand the customer's needs, wants, and concerns on a deeper level. It also helps the salesperson to build trust and rapport with the customer by showing that they understand and care about their feelings and experiences.

Empathetic listening can be demonstrated through verbal and nonverbal cues, such as:

Reflecting on the customer's feelings and experiences

Responding with understanding and validation

Using a calm and supportive tone of voice

Maintaining eye contact and open body language

Avoiding interrupting or judging the customer

For example, a customer is speaking with a salesperson about a recent loss of a family member and the customer is expressing sadness and grief. The salesperson uses empathetic listening by reflecting the customer's feelings, responding with understanding and validation, and using a calm and supportive tone of voice. The salesperson also offers condolences and shows that they understand and care about the customer's feelings and experiences.

Empathetic listening can be beneficial in a sales context as it can help to build trust and rapport with the customer, to understand the customer's needs and wants on a deeper level, and to improve communication and customer satisfaction. This can ultimately lead to more successful sales outcomes as it demonstrates that the salesperson cares about the customer's well-being.

Reflecting on the customer's feelings and experiences

Reflecting on the customer's feelings and experiences is a key aspect of empathetic listening. It involves restating or paraphrasing what the customer has said, in order to show that you have understood their feelings and perspective. Reflecting on the customer's feelings and experiences also helps to acknowledge and validate their emotions.

There are different ways to reflect on the customer's feelings and experiences, such as:

Paraphrasing: Restating the customer's words in your own words, to confirm your understanding of what they have said.

Reflecting feelings: Identifying and naming the emotions that the customer is expressing.

Reflecting content: Restating the key points of what the customer has said, to confirm your understanding of their message.

For example, a customer is speaking with a salesperson about a recent loss of a family member and the customer is expressing sadness and grief. The salesperson uses reflection by saying something like "I can hear that you're feeling really upset and sad about your loss" which validates the customer's feelings and shows that they understand and care about the customer's feelings and experiences.

A second example of reflecting on the customer's feelings and experiences in a sales context:

A customer is speaking with a salesperson about a new service, and they express uncertainty about the service's ability to meet their needs. The salesperson uses reflection by saying something like "It sounds like you're not sure if this service will meet your needs." This not only confirms the salesperson's understanding of the customer's perspective but also acknowledges the customer's uncertainty and allows the salesperson to understand the customer's concerns.

By using reflecting, the salesperson is able to understand the customer's perspective and concerns, and can then offer more information or examples that might better address the customer's uncertainty. This can help to build trust and rapport with the customer by showing that the salesperson understands and cares about their needs and concerns.

In this example, reflecting allows the salesperson to understand the customer's concerns, and to provide more information that can help to address the customer's uncertainty and increase the chances of closing a sale. It also allows the customer to feel heard and understood which can ultimately lead to a more positive and successful customer experience.

Here's a third example of reflecting on the customer's feelings and experiences in a sales context:

A customer is speaking with a salesperson about a new product, and they express excitement about the product's features but have some doubts about the product's price. The salesperson uses reflecting by saying something like "It sounds like you're really excited about the features of the product, but you have some concerns about the price." This not only confirms the salesperson's understanding of the customer's perspective but also acknowledges the customer's mixed feelings and concerns.

By using reflecting, the salesperson is able to understand the customer's perspective, both positive and negative, and can then offer options or alternatives that might help the customer to overcome their concerns. This can help to build trust and rapport with the customer by showing that the salesperson understands and cares about their needs and concerns.

In this example, reflecting allows the salesperson to understand the customer's concerns, and to provide more information or options that can help to address the customer's concerns and increase the chances of closing a sale. It also allows the customer to feel heard and understood which can ultimately lead to a more positive and successful customer experience. Reflecting on the customer's feelings and experiences is a powerful tool for salespeople to improve communication, build trust and rapport with customers, and ultimately close more sales.

Reflecting on the customer's feelings and experiences is an important aspect of empathetic listening, as it allows the salesperson to understand the customer's needs, wants, and concerns on a deeper level, and to build trust and rapport with the customer. It also shows that the salesperson cares about the customer's well-being and is more likely to lead to a positive outcome for the sales process.

Responding with understanding and validation

Responding with understanding and validation is another key aspect of empathetic listening. It involves acknowledging and accepting the customer's feelings, rather than trying to change or fix them. This helps to show the customer that their feelings and experiences are understood and valued.

There are different ways to respond with understanding and validation, such as:

Acknowledging the customer's feelings: Saying something like "I understand how you feel" or "I can see why you're upset."

Validating the customer's feelings: Saying something like "It's understandable that you feel that way" or "Your feelings make sense."

Offering support: Saying something like "I'm here to help" or "Is there anything I can do to assist you?"

For example, a customer is speaking with a salesperson about a new product and they express frustration with the product's lack of features. The salesperson responds with understanding and validation by saying something like "I understand that you're frustrated with the product's lack of features. I can see how that would be disappointing." This not only acknowledges the customer's feelings but also validates their frustration and shows that the salesperson understands and cares about the customer's needs and concerns.

Responding with understanding and validation can be beneficial in a sales context as it can help to build trust and rapport with the customer, to understand the customer's needs and wants on a deeper level, and to improve communication and customer satisfaction. This can ultimately lead to more successful sales outcomes as it demonstrates that the salesperson cares about the customer's well-being and is interested in finding a solution that meets their needs.

Here's a second example of responding with understanding and validation in a sales context:

A customer is speaking with a salesperson about a new service, and they express uncertainty about the service's ability to meet their needs. The salesperson responds with understanding and validation by saying something like "I understand that you're uncertain if this service will meet your needs. It's understandable that you would want to make sure this service will meet your needs before making a decision." This not only acknowledges the customer's feelings and concerns but also validates them and shows that the salesperson is willing to help and understand the customer's needs.

By responding with understanding and validation, the salesperson is able to show the customer that they care about their needs and concerns and that they are willing to help. This can help to build trust and rapport with the customer and ultimately lead to the outcome of a more successful sale.

It's important to note that responding with understanding and validation should be done in an authentic way, rather than in a scripted way, as it helps to build trust and rapport with the customer. It also helps to show that the salesperson is genuinely interested in understanding the customer's needs, which can lead to a better understanding of the customer's needs and ultimately to the outcome of a more positive and successful sale.

Here's a third example of responding with understanding and validation in a sales context:

A customer is speaking with a salesperson about a new product, and they express concerns about the product's price. The salesperson responds with understanding and validation by saying something like "I understand that the price of the product is a concern for you. It's understandable that you want to make sure you're getting the best value for your money." This not only acknowledges the customer's feelings and concerns but also validates them and shows that the salesperson understands and cares about the customer's needs and concerns.

By responding with understanding and validation, the salesperson is able to show the customer that they care about their needs and concerns and that they are willing to help. This can help to build trust and rapport with the customer and ultimately lead to the outcome of a more successful sale.

It's important to note that responding with understanding and validation should be done in an authentic way, rather than in a scripted way, as it helps to build trust and rapport with the customer. It also helps to show that the salesperson is genuinely interested in understanding the customer's needs, which can lead to a better understanding of the customer's needs and ultimately to the outcome of a more positive and successful sale.

Using a calm and supportive tone of voice

Using a calm and supportive tone of voice is an important aspect of effective communication, particularly in a sales context. It helps to create a positive and relaxed atmosphere and can make the customer feel more at ease and willing to engage in conversation.

A calm and supportive tone of voice can be characterized by:

A slow and steady pace: Speak at a moderate pace, taking pauses as needed. Avoid speaking too quickly or too slowly.

A moderate volume: Speak at a level that is comfortable for the customer, not too loudly or too softly.

A friendly and approachable tone: Use a tone that is friendly and welcoming, rather than aggressive or confrontational.

For example, a salesperson can use a calm and supportive tone of voice when a customer expresses concerns about the product's price. The salesperson can say something like "I understand that the price of the product is a concern for you. I'd be happy to go over the pricing options with you and explain how the product's features and benefits can justify the cost. Can we take a look at that together?" This sentence shows understanding, willingness to help and it's spoken in a calm and supportive tone.

Using a calm and supportive tone of voice can be beneficial in a sales context because it can help to build trust and rapport with the customer, to create a positive and relaxed atmosphere, and to improve communication and customer satisfaction. It can also help the customer to feel at ease, which can lead to more successful sales outcomes.

Maintaining eye contact and open body language

Maintaining eye contact and open body language is an important aspect of effective communication, particularly in a sales context. It helps to create a sense of connection and engagement with the customer and can make the customer feel more at ease and willing to engage in conversation.

Eye contact: Maintaining eye contact during a conversation is a sign of attentiveness and engagement. It can also help to build trust and rapport with the customer. However, it's important to be aware of cultural differences, in some cultures maintaining eye contact may be considered rude or disrespectful, so it's important to be aware of and sensitive to these differences.

Open body language: Open body language involves maintaining an open and relaxed posture, facing the customer directly, and using gestures and facial expressions that are appropriate to the conversation. This can include things like nodding in agreement, smiling, and leaning in slightly when engaged in conversation.

For example, a salesperson can maintain eye contact and open body language when a customer expresses concerns about the product's price. The salesperson can maintain eye contact with the customer while nodding and saying something like "I understand that the price of the product is a concern for you. I'd be happy to go over the pricing options with you and explain how the product's features and benefits can justify the cost." While saying this, the salesperson can also use open body language such as facing the customer directly, making gestures with hands to show a willingness to help, and having an open and relaxed posture.

Maintaining eye contact and open body language can be beneficial in a sales context because it can help to build trust and rapport with the customer, create a sense of connection and engagement, and improve communication and customer satisfaction. It also helps the customer to feel that the salesperson is attentive, engaged, and interested in their needs, which can lead to more successful sales outcomes.

Avoiding interrupting or judging the customer

Avoiding interrupting or judging the customer is an important aspect of effective communication, particularly in a sales context. Interrupting or judging the customer can come across as disrespectful or dismissive and can create a negative atmosphere that can damage trust and rapport with the customer.

Avoid interrupting: Interrupting the customer can come across as rude and dismissive, it can also prevent the customer from fully expressing themselves and their concerns. It's important to give the customer space to speak and express their thoughts and feelings.

Avoid judging: Judging the customer can come across as arrogant and dismissive and can make the customer feel unheard and dismissed. It's important to listen to the customer without judging their thoughts and feelings and to be respectful of their perspective.

For example, a salesperson should avoid interrupting a customer when they are expressing concerns about the product's price, instead, the salesperson should allow the customer to fully express themselves, and then respond with understanding and validation. The salesperson should also avoid judging the customer's concerns as unimportant or irrelevant, instead, they should show respect for the customer's perspective and take it into consideration when addressing their concerns.

Avoiding interrupting or judging the customer can be beneficial in a sales context because it can help to build trust and rapport with the customer, create a positive and relaxed atmosphere, and to improve communication and customer satisfaction. It also helps the customer to feel heard and respected, which can lead to more successful sales outcomes.

Sure, here's a second example of avoiding interrupting or judging the customer in a sales context:

A customer is speaking with a salesperson about a new product, and they express concerns about the product's functionality. The salesperson avoids interrupting the customer by allowing them to fully express their concerns and ask questions. Instead of judging the customer's concerns as unimportant or irrelevant, the salesperson responds with understanding and validation, saying something like "I understand that the functionality of the product is a concern for you. Let me explain how the product works and address any specific concerns you may have. Can we go over that together?" This response not only shows an understanding of the customer's concerns but also the willingness to help and offer solutions.

By avoiding interrupting or judging the customer, the salesperson is able to show the customer that they care about their needs and concerns and that they are willing to help. This can help to build trust and rapport with the customer and ultimately lead to the outcome of a more successful sale.

Here's a third example of avoiding interrupting or judging the customer in a sales context:

A customer is speaking with a salesperson about a new service, and they express concerns about the service's reliability. The salesperson avoids interrupting the customer by allowing them to fully express their concerns and ask questions. Instead of judging the customer's concerns as unimportant or irrelevant, the salesperson responds with understanding and validation, saying something like "I understand that the reliability of the service is a concern for you. Let me provide you with some data and testimonials from our satisfied customers that demonstrate the reliability of our service. Can we go over that together?" This response not only shows an understanding of the customer's concerns but also a willingness to help and offer solutions.

By avoiding interrupting or judging the customer, the salesperson is able to show the customer that they care about their needs and concerns and that they are willing to help. This can help to build trust and rapport with the customer and ultimately lead to the outcome of a more successful sale.

Critical listening

Critical listening is a type of active listening that requires the listener to evaluate and analyze the information being presented, rather than simply accepting it at face value. It involves paying attention to both the content and the context of the message and considering the speaker's perspective and potential biases.

Critical listening can be used in a sales context to help the salesperson fully understand the customer's needs and concerns and to respond in an appropriate and effective way. When listening critically, the salesperson should pay attention to:

The content of the message: What is the customer actually saying? What are their needs and concerns?

The context of the message: What is the situation or context in which the message is being given? How might this be influencing the customer's perspective?

The speaker's perspective and biases: What is the customer's background, experience, and position? How might this be influencing their perspective?

By practicing critical listening, the salesperson can gain a deeper understanding of the customer's needs and concerns and can respond in a more appropriate and effective way. This can help to build trust and rapport with the customer, and can ultimately lead to the outcome of a more successful sale.

It's also important to be aware that critical listening is not the same as being skeptical or cynical, it's a more analytical, thoughtful, and effective way of listening. It can be used to challenge assumptions and gain a deeper understanding of the situation.

Critical listening involves using a set of analytical skills to evaluate and understand the information being presented. It requires the listener to be more engaged and active in the listening process and to consider multiple perspectives.

When listening critically, the salesperson should be aware of their own biases and assumptions and try to set them aside. This can help them to gain a more objective understanding of the customer's needs and concerns.

For example, a customer may be expressing concerns about the cost of a product, and the salesperson with critical listening skills would not only hear the words that the customer is saying, but also consider the context in which the customer is speaking, such as their budget, priorities, and goals. The salesperson then can help the customer to understand how the product can address their needs and how it aligns with their priorities, this can help the customer to see the value of the product and to make a purchase decision that is right for them.

Additionally, critical listening also involves questioning the information being presented and seeking clarification when needed. This can help to ensure that the salesperson fully understands the customer's needs and concerns, and can respond in an appropriate and effective way.

In summary, critical listening is an important skill for salespeople to develop. It can help them to build trust and rapport with the customer, to gain a deeper understanding of the customer's needs and concerns, and to respond in an appropriate and effective way. This can ultimately lead to more successful sales outcomes.

Here's an example of critical listening in a sales context:

A customer is speaking with a salesperson about a new product, and they express concerns about the product's durability. The salesperson, using critical listening skills, listens carefully to the customer's concerns and asks questions to gain a deeper understanding of the customer's needs. They also consider the context of the customer's message, such as the customer's previous experiences and the intended usage of the product.

The salesperson then responds in an appropriate and effective way by acknowledging the customer's concerns and providing additional information about the product's durability. For example, the salesperson might say something like "I understand that durability is a concern for you. I want to make sure you have all the information you need to make an informed decision. Our product has undergone rigorous testing and has been proven to be highly durable in similar usage scenarios. Can I provide you with more detailed information and data to back that up?"

By practicing critical listening, the salesperson is able to gain a deeper understanding of the customer's needs and concerns and respond in a way that addresses those concerns directly. This can help to build trust and rapport with the customer, and can ultimately lead to the outcome of a more successful sale.

Here's a second example of critical listening in a sales context:

A customer is speaking with a salesperson about a new service, and they express concerns about the service's reliability. The salesperson, using critical listening skills, listens carefully to the customer's concerns and asks questions to gain a deeper understanding of the customer's needs. They also consider the context of the customer's message, such as their previous experiences with similar services and their expectations for this service.

The salesperson then responds in an appropriate and effective way by acknowledging the customer's concerns and providing additional information about the service's reliability. For example, the salesperson might say something like "I understand that reliability is a concern for you. I want to make sure you have all the information you need to make an informed decision. Our service has been used by many satisfied customers and has a proven track record of reliability. Can I provide you with some customer testimonials and statistics to back that up?"

By practicing critical listening, the salesperson is able to gain a deeper understanding of the customer's needs and concerns and respond in a way that addresses those concerns directly. This can help to build trust and rapport with the customer, and can ultimately lead to the outcome of a more successful sale.

Here's a third example of critical listening in a sales context:

A customer is speaking with a salesperson about new software, and they express concerns about the software's compatibility with their current systems. The salesperson, using critical listening skills, listens carefully to the customer's concerns and asks questions to gain a deeper understanding of the customer's needs. They also consider the context of the customer's message, such as their current systems and their future plans for the business.

The salesperson then responds in an appropriate and effective way by acknowledging the customer's concerns and providing additional information about the software's compatibility. For example, the salesperson might say something like "I understand that compatibility is a concern for you. I want to make sure you have all the information you need to make an informed decision. Our software has been designed to be compatible with a wide range of systems and it has been tested to work seamlessly with similar systems as yours. Can I provide you with more detailed information and a demonstration of how it works with your current systems?"

By practicing critical listening, the salesperson is able to gain a deeper understanding of the customer's needs and concerns and respond in a way that addresses those concerns directly. This can help to build trust and rapport with the customer, and can ultimately lead to the outcome of a more successful sale.

Reflective listening

Reflective listening is a technique that involves listening to a speaker and then restating or paraphrasing what they have said in order to show that you have understood and acknowledged their message. It is a way of demonstrating active listening and encouraging the speaker to continue sharing their thoughts and feelings.

In the sales context, reflective listening can be used to build trust and rapport with customers by showing that you understand and care about their needs and concerns. It can also help the salesperson to gain a deeper understanding of the customer's perspective, which can inform more effective solutions.

An example of reflective listening in a sales context might be as follows:

A customer is speaking with a salesperson about a new product, and they express concerns about the product's features. The salesperson listens carefully to the customer's concerns and reflects back on what they have heard, by saying something like "I understand that you have some concerns about the product's features, specifically about X, Y, and Z. Is that correct?" This not only shows that the salesperson is actively listening to the customer but also allows the customer to correct or elaborate on their concerns if needed.

Here's a second example of reflective listening in a sales context:

A customer is speaking with a salesperson about a new service, and they express concerns about the service's flexibility. The salesperson listens carefully to the customer's concerns and reflects back on what they have heard, by saying something like "I understand that you're looking for a service that can accommodate your changing needs and be flexible. You want to be able to adjust the service as your business evolves, is that correct?" This not only shows that the salesperson is actively listening to the customer but also allows the customer to correct or elaborate on their concerns if needed.

By using reflective listening, the salesperson is able to build trust and rapport with the customer, as well as gain a deeper understanding of the customer's needs and concerns. This can ultimately lead to more effective solutions, such as offering a service that can be customized to the customer's specific needs and being able to tailor the service based on the customer's feedback.

Here is a third example of reflective listening in a sales context:

A customer is speaking with a salesperson about a new product, and they express concerns about the product's compatibility with their existing system. The salesperson listens carefully to the customer's concerns and reflects back on what they have heard, by saying something like "I understand that you're concerned about how well this product will integrate with your current setup. Specifically, you want to make sure it will work seamlessly with the software and hardware you already have in place, is that correct?" This not only shows that the salesperson is actively listening to the customer but also allows the customer to correct or elaborate on their concerns if needed.

By using reflective listening, the salesperson is able to build trust and rapport with the customer, as well as gain a deeper understanding of the customer's needs and concerns. This can ultimately lead to more effective solutions, such as offering a product that is compatible with the customer's existing systems or providing technical support to help the customer with the integration process.

By using reflective listening, the salesperson is able to build trust and rapport with the customer, as well as gain a deeper understanding of the customer's needs and concerns. This can ultimately lead to more effective solutions and a higher chance of closing a sale.

Summarizing

Summarizing is a technique that involves condensing and simplifying a speaker's message in order to understand and retain the main points. It can be used in a variety of settings, including sales, to help the listener understand the speaker's message more effectively.

In the sales context, summarizing can be used to help the salesperson understand the customer's needs and concerns more clearly. It can also be used to help the customer understand the salesperson's proposal or solution more clearly.

For example, a customer may speak at length about their needs and concerns, and a salesperson can use summarizing to restate the main points in a clear and concise way. This can help the customer to see that the salesperson has understood their needs and concerns, and it can also help the salesperson to articulate their proposal in a way that addresses those needs and concerns more effectively.

A customer is speaking with a salesperson about a new product, and they express a variety of different needs and concerns. The customer mentions that they are looking for a product that is easy to use, has a good warranty, and is affordable. They also express concerns about compatibility with their existing system and the level of customer support provided.

The salesperson uses summarizing to restate the main points of the customer's message in a clear and concise way. For example, the salesperson might say something like "So, to summarize, you're looking for a product that is easy to use, has a good warranty, and is affordable. You also have concerns about compatibility with your existing system and the level of customer support provided."

By summarizing the customer's message, the salesperson is able to demonstrate that they have understood the customer's needs and concerns and are able to articulate them in a clear and concise way. This can help to build trust and rapport with the customer and can ultimately lead to the outcome of a more successful sale.

Summarizing can be done verbally or in writing, it's an effective technique to make sure that all parties are on the same page and that the main points of the conversation are well understood.

Summarizing can also be used during the negotiation process in sales, to ensure that both parties have a clear understanding of the main points being discussed and agreed upon.

CHAPTER THREE

Overcoming Barriers to Listening in Sales

Common obstacles to effective listening in sales

Effective listening is an important skill in sales, but it can be challenging to achieve due to a variety of obstacles. Identifying and addressing these obstacles can help salespeople to become better listeners and ultimately improve their sales performance.

Here are some common obstacles to effective listening in sales and some suggestions for addressing them:

Preoccupation: Salespeople may be preoccupied with their own thoughts and concerns, which can make it difficult for them to focus on what the customer is saying. To address this, salespeople can practice mindfulness and focus exercises to help them stay present in the conversation.

Assumptions: Salespeople may make assumptions about the customer's needs and concerns based on their own experiences or biases, which can lead to misunderstandings. To address this, salespeople can practice active listening and ask questions to gain a deeper understanding of the customer's needs and concerns.

Interrupting: Salespeople may interrupt the customer or talk over them, which can show disrespect and prevent the customer from fully expressing their thoughts and feelings. To address this, salespeople can practice active listening and refrain from interrupting the customer.

Judgment: Salespeople may judge the customer based on their appearance, accent, or other factors, which can lead to misunderstandings and can also lead to the loss of potential clients. To address this, salespeople can practice empathy and refrain from making assumptions or judgments about the customer.

Distractions: Salespeople may be easily distracted by their surroundings, such as noise, notifications, or other distractions which can make it difficult to pay attention to the customer. To address this, salespeople can choose an appropriate environment for the conversation, minimize distractions, and if needed, use noise-canceling headphones.

By identifying and addressing common obstacles to effective listening in sales, salespeople can improve their ability to listen to and understand their customers, which can ultimately lead to more successful sales outcomes.

Preoccupation & Listening

Preoccupation refers to being absorbed in one's own thoughts or concerns, rather than being fully present and engaged in a conversation. It can be a major obstacle to effective listening in sales, as it can make it difficult for salespeople to focus on what the customer is saying and to understand their needs and concerns.

There are a few reasons why salespeople may be preoccupied during a conversation. For example, they may be worried about their own performance or the outcome of the sale, or they may be thinking about other things going on in their personal or professional life. Additionally, if a salesperson has had a previous conversation with a customer that didn't go well, it may affect their mindset during the next conversation.

To address preoccupation, salespeople can practice mindfulness and focus exercises. Mindfulness is the practice of paying attention to the present moment, non-judgmentally. Salespeople can practice mindfulness by focusing on their breath, the sensation of their body, or the sound of the customer's voice. This can help them to stay present in the conversation and to focus on what the customer is saying.

Additionally, Salespeople can also try to clear their minds before having a conversation with a customer. This can be done by taking a deep breath, taking a walk, or doing a quick exercise.

Another way to address preoccupation is to set an intention before the conversation. By setting a clear intention, salespeople can focus on the goals of the conversation and the customer's needs and concerns. This can help them to stay focused and engaged during the conversation.

By addressing preoccupation and practicing mindfulness, salespeople can improve their ability to listen to and understand their customers, which can ultimately lead to more successful sales outcomes.

Here are a few more things to consider when addressing preoccupation in the context of sales:

1. Prioritizing listening: Salespeople can make a conscious effort to prioritize listening during conversations with customers. This means giving the customer their full attention and making sure to actively listen to what they are saying.
2. Reflecting on past conversations: Salespeople can reflect on past conversations with customers that didn't go well and try to identify any patterns or areas where they might have been preoccupied. This can help them to be more aware of their own preoccupation in the future and take steps to address them.
3. Taking notes: Salespeople can take notes during conversations with customers as a way to stay focused and engaged. This can also help them to remember important details and to follow up effectively.
4. Asking questions: Asking open-ended questions can help salespeople to gain a deeper understanding of the customer's needs and concerns. It also shows that you are paying attention and that you are engaged in the conversation.
5. Follow-up: Following up with customers after a conversation can help salespeople to stay engaged and focused. It also helps them to remember important details and to build stronger relationships with customers.

The preoccupation can be a difficult obstacle to overcome, but by being mindful of it, and taking steps to address it, salespeople can improve their ability to listen and understand their customers, which can ultimately lead to more successful sales outcomes.

Assumptions and Listening

Making assumptions can be a major obstacle to effective listening in sales, as it can lead to misunderstandings between the salesperson and the customer. Assumptions are beliefs or ideas that are accepted as true without being verified or proven. In sales, assumptions can be made about a customer's needs, wants, concerns, or decision-making process, based on limited information or past experiences.

For example, a salesperson may assume that a customer is not interested in a product because they are not asking many questions, when in fact, the customer is just a more reserved person. Or, the salesperson may assume that a customer is price-sensitive, when in fact, the customer is more interested in the quality of the product.

Here are a few ways to address assumptions when it comes to listening in sales:

1. Ask open-ended questions: Salespeople can ask open-ended questions that encourage customers to share more information about their needs, wants, and concerns. This can help salespeople to gain a deeper understanding of the customer and to avoid making assumptions.
2. Listen actively: Salespeople can practice active listening, which means listening with the intent to understand the customer's message and to respond appropriately. This can help salespeople to avoid making assumptions and to focus on the customer's needs and concerns.
3. Reflect on past assumptions: Salespeople can reflect on past assumptions they made with customers and consider how they might have affected the outcome of the conversation. This can help them to be more aware of their assumptions in the future.
4. Seek feedback: Salespeople can seek feedback from customers about their listening skills and ask for constructive criticism. This can help them to understand where they might be making assumptions, and help them to improve their listening skills.
5. Practice empathy: Salespeople can practice empathy, which means trying to understand and share the feelings of the customer. This can help salespeople to avoid making assumptions and to build stronger relationships with customers.

Addressing assumptions can be a key to effective listening in sales, as it can lead to a deeper understanding of the customer's needs and concerns, and ultimately to more successful sales outcomes.

Interrupting and Sales

Interrupting can be a major obstacle to effective listening in sales, as it can make it difficult for salespeople to fully understand the customer's needs and concerns. Interrupting refers to cutting off or interrupting someone while they are speaking, which can make it difficult for the listener to understand the speaker's message and can also make the speaker feel disrespected or unimportant.

In sales, interrupting can occur when a salesperson is too focused on making a sale or on their own agenda, rather than fully listening to the customer. Interrupting can also occur when a salesperson is not fully present and engaged in the conversation, and is instead preoccupied with their own thoughts or concerns.

Here are a few ways to address interrupting when it comes to listening in sales:

Wait for the customer to finish speaking: Salespeople can practice active listening by waiting for the customer to finish speaking before responding or asking follow-up questions. This shows that the salesperson is fully engaged in the conversation and is interested in what the customer has to say.

Use nonverbal cues: Salespeople can use nonverbal cues, such as nodding and maintaining eye contact, to signal that they are actively listening and engaged in the conversation.

Reflect on the conversation: Salespeople can reflect on the conversation and consider if they interrupted the customer at any point. This can help them to be more aware of their tendency to interrupt in the future.

Seek feedback: Salespeople can seek feedback from customers about their listening skills and ask for constructive criticism. This can help them to understand where they might be interrupting, and help them to improve their listening skills.

Practice mindfulness: Salespeople can practice mindfulness, which means being present and engaged in the moment, this can help them to stay focused and avoid interrupting.

By addressing interrupting and practicing active listening, salespeople can improve their ability to listen to and understand their customers, which can ultimately lead to more successful sales outcomes.

Judgment and Sales

Judging can be a major obstacle to effective listening in sales, as it can lead to misunderstandings and can make it difficult for salespeople to fully understand the customer's needs and concerns. Judging refers to forming an opinion or evaluation about someone or something based on limited information or past experiences. In sales, judging can occur when a salesperson makes assumptions about a customer based on their appearance, manner of speaking, or other superficial factors.

For example, a salesperson may judge a customer as uninterested or not having the ability to afford a product based on their dress or appearance, when in fact, the customer is genuinely interested and has the financial means to purchase the product.

Here are a few ways to address judging when it comes to listening in sales:

1. Practice empathy: Salespeople can practice empathy, which means trying to understand and share the feelings of the customer. This can

help salespeople to avoid judging and to build stronger relationships with customers.

2. Be mindful of assumptions: Salespeople can be mindful of their assumptions and be aware of their own biases. This can help them to avoid judging and to focus on the customer's needs and concerns.

3. Listen actively: Salespeople can practice active listening, which means listening with the intent to understand the customer's message and to respond appropriately. This can help salespeople to avoid judging and to focus on the customer's needs and concerns.

4. Reflect on past experiences: Salespeople can reflect on past experiences where they may have judged a customer and consider how it might have affected the outcome of the conversation. This can help them to be more aware of their tendency to judge in the future.

5. Seek feedback: Salespeople can seek feedback from customers about their listening skills and ask for constructive criticism. This can help them to understand where they might be judging, and help them to improve their listening skills.

By addressing judging and practicing empathy and active listening, salespeople can improve their ability to listen to and understand their customers, which can ultimately lead to more successful sales outcomes.

Distractions & Sales

Distractions can be a major obstacle to effective listening in sales, as they can make it difficult for salespeople to fully focus on and understand the customer's needs and concerns. Distractions can come in many forms, such as external distractions like noise or interruptions, or internal distractions like preoccupation with one's own thoughts or concerns.

In sales, distractions can occur when a salesperson is multitasking, checking their phone or email, or thinking about their next appointment or task. Distractions can also occur when a salesperson is not fully present and engaged in the conversation, and is instead preoccupied with their own thoughts or concerns.

Here are a few ways to address distractions when it comes to listening in sales:

Minimize external distractions: Salespeople can minimize external distractions by finding a quiet and private space to conduct sales meetings. They can also ask customers to refrain from using their phones or other electronic devices during the meeting.

1. Practice mindfulness: Salespeople can practice mindfulness, which means being present and engaged in the moment. This can help them to stay focused and avoid distractions.
2. Prioritize the customer: Salespeople can prioritize the customer by giving them their full attention during the sales meeting. This can help them to avoid distractions and to focus on the customer's needs and concerns.
3. Reflect on the conversation: Salespeople can reflect on the conversation and consider if they were distracted at any point. This can help them to be more aware of their tendency to be distracted in the future.
4. Seek feedback: Salespeople can seek feedback from customers about their listening skills and ask for constructive criticism. This can help them to understand where they might be distracted, and help them to improve their listening skills.

By addressing distractions and practicing mindfulness and active listening, salespeople can improve their ability to listen to and understand their customers, which can ultimately lead to more successful sales outcomes.

CHAPTER FOUR

Active Listening Techniques in Sales

Techniques for actively engaging with customers

Introducing and demonstrating techniques for actively engaging with customers, such as paraphrasing, reflecting, and summarizing.

Actively engaging with customers is an important aspect of effective listening in sales, as it helps salespeople to fully understand the customer's needs and concerns. Actively engaging with customers can involve a variety of techniques, such as asking open-ended questions, paraphrasing and summarizing, and using reflective listening.

Here are a few examples of techniques that can be used to actively engage with customers:

Open-ended questions: Salespeople can use open-ended questions, such as "Can you tell me more about..." or "How do you feel about...," to encourage customers to share more information about their needs and concerns.

Paraphrasing and summarizing: Salespeople can paraphrase and summarize what the customer has said to ensure that they have fully understood the customer's message. This can help to build trust and deepen the customer's engagement with the salesperson.

Reflective listening: Salespeople can use reflective listening, which involves repeating back to the customer what they have said in their own words, this can help to build trust and show the customer that they are being heard.

Active engagement prompts: Salespeople can use active engagement prompts such as "What do you think?", "Can you tell me more about that?", or "How does that make you feel?" to keep the customer talking and to encourage them to share more information.

Acknowledgment: Salespeople can use nonverbal cues such as nodding or making affirmations such as "I see" or "I understand" to show the customer that they are actively engaged in the conversation.

Building rapport: Salespeople can build rapport with customers by finding common ground, showing genuine interest, and being empathetic. Building rapport with customers can help to create a sense of trust and can make the customer feel more comfortable sharing their needs and concerns.

Active listening: Salespeople can use active listening techniques such as paraphrasing, summarizing, and reflective listening to ensure that they fully understand the customer's needs and concerns. This can help salespeople to identify customer needs and tailor their approach accordingly.

Asking open-ended questions: Salespeople can use open-ended questions to encourage customers to share more information about their needs and concerns. This can help salespeople to gather more information about customer needs and tailor their approach accordingly.

Using Visual aids: Salespeople can use visual aids such as brochures, product demonstrations, or videos to help customers understand the features and benefits of the products or services. This can help to engage customers and build interest in the products or services.

Following up: Salespeople can follow up with customers after the initial conversation to show that they are interested in customer needs and concerns. This can help to build trust and customer loyalty.

By introducing and demonstrating techniques for actively engaging with customers, salespeople can improve their ability to listen to and understand their customers, which can ultimately lead to more successful sales outcomes. Additionally, it's important to note that the key to actively engaging with customers is to be genuine, authentic, and truly interested in understanding the customer's needs and concerns.

By actively engaging with customers, salespeople can improve their ability to understand customer needs and concerns, which can ultimately lead to more successful sales outcomes. Additionally, actively engaging with customers can also help to create a positive relationship with customers, which can lead to repeat business and increase the chances of customer referral.

CHAPTER FIVE

Empathetic Listening in Sales

Concept of empathy

Empathy is the ability to understand and share the feelings of another person. It involves the ability to put oneself in another person's shoes and to understand their perspective. Empathy is an important part of effective communication, as it allows people to connect with and understand each other on a deeper level.

There are different types of empathy, including:

Cognitive empathy: This is the ability to understand another person's thoughts and feelings, without necessarily feeling the same way. This type of empathy allows people to understand and predict the behavior of others.

Emotional empathy: This is the ability to feel the emotions of another person as if they were one's own. This type of empathy allows people to connect with others on a deeper emotional level, and to feel compassion for others.

Compassionate empathy: This is the ability to understand the feelings of others and to respond with care and concern. This type of empathy leads to actions that help to alleviate the suffering of others.

Empathy is important in sales because it allows salespeople to understand the needs and concerns of their customers, which can help them to tailor their approach and make a sale. Salespeople can use empathy to build trust with customers and to create positive relationships. Additionally, salespeople who are empathetic and compassionate can more effectively identify the customer's pain points and offer the right solution.

Empathy can also be important in conflict resolution, as it allows people to understand the perspective of the other person and to find a solution that meets the needs of both parties.

It's important to note that empathy is a skill that can be developed and improved with practice. Salespeople and anyone else looking to improve their empathy can do so by practicing active listening, asking open-ended questions, and trying to see things from the other person's perspective. Additionally, they can try to cultivate an empathetic mindset by taking the time to understand the feelings of others and responding with care and concern.

Cognitive empathy and listening

Cognitive empathy, also known as perspective-taking, is the ability to understand and appreciate the thoughts, feelings, and intentions of others, without necessarily feeling the same way. This type of empathy is important in the context of listening, as it allows the listener to understand where the speaker is coming from and to appreciate their perspective.

When a salesperson uses cognitive empathy, they can better understand the customer's needs and concerns, even if they don't necessarily agree with them. This understanding can help the salesperson to tailor their approach and to make a more effective sales pitch. For example, if a customer is hesitant to buy a product because they're worried about the cost, a salesperson who uses cognitive empathy can understand the customer's perspective and can offer solutions that help the customer to see how the product can save them money in the long run.

Additionally, cognitive empathy can also be applied to understanding the customer's buying motivation and tailoring the pitch accordingly. For example, if a customer is motivated by the idea of being socially responsible, a salesperson can highlight how the product or service they are offering aligns with this motivation.

In summary, cognitive empathy is an important aspect of listening, as it allows the listener to understand the perspective of the speaker, and to better understand their needs, concerns, and motivations. Salespeople who can use cognitive empathy can more effectively understand and meet the needs of their customers, which can lead to more successful sales outcomes.

Emotional empathy and listening

Emotional empathy, also known as affective empathy, is the ability to share and understand the emotions of others. This type of empathy is important in the context of listening, as it allows the listener to connect with the speaker on an emotional level and show that they care.

When a salesperson uses emotional empathy, they can build trust and a deeper connection with their customer. They can show that they understand and care about their customer's feelings, which can make the customer feel more comfortable and willing to share more information. For example, if a customer is upset about a recent negative experience with a similar product or service, a salesperson who uses emotional empathy can acknowledge the customer's feelings and offer support and understanding, rather than just trying to make a sale.

Additionally, emotional empathy can also help a salesperson to identify the customer's pain points and tailor the pitch accordingly. For example, if a customer is feeling stressed about a recent change in their life, a salesperson who uses emotional empathy can identify this stress and offer a solution that helps the customer to feel more in control.

In summary, emotional empathy is an important aspect of listening, as it allows the listener to connect with the speaker on an emotional level and show that they care. Salespeople who can use emotional empathy can build trust and a deeper connection with their customers, which can lead to more successful sales outcomes. They can also identify the customer's pain points and tailor the pitch accordingly.

Compassionate empathy and listening

Compassionate empathy, also known as an empathetic concern, is the ability to understand and share the feelings of others, and to respond with a desire to help. It's a combination of cognitive and emotional empathy, where not only the salesperson can understand and share the feelings of their customer but also act to alleviate their suffering.

When a salesperson uses compassionate empathy, they can not only build trust and connection with their customer but also create a sense of value and belonging. They can show that they understand the customer's situation and are willing to take action to help them. For example, if a customer is looking for a solution to a specific problem, a salesperson who uses compassionate empathy can take the time to understand the customer's situation and offer a personalized solution that addresses the customer's specific needs.

Additionally, compassionate empathy can also help salespeople to understand the customer's values, goals, and priorities. It allows them to tailor the pitch not only to meet the customer's needs but also to align with their values and priorities. This can create a sense of trust and value for the customer, which can increase the chances of customer loyalty.

In summary, compassionate empathy is an advanced form of empathy that involves understanding, sharing, and responding to the feelings of others. Salespeople who can use compassionate empathy can not only build trust and connection with their customers, but also create a sense of value and belonging, and offer personalized solutions that align with the customer's values and priorities.

Empathy and Trust

Empathy and trust are closely related concepts in that empathy can help to build trust, and trust can help to foster empathy.

Empathy can help to build trust by allowing people to understand and connect with others on a deeper level. When a salesperson can understand the needs and concerns of their customer, and respond with compassion and understanding, it can help to build trust between the salesperson and the customer. Trust is important in sales, as customers are more likely to buy from someone they trust. Trust also makes it more likely that the customer will be willing to share more information with the salesperson, which can help the salesperson to better understand the customer's needs and tailor their approach accordingly.

On the other hand, trust can help to foster empathy as well, when people trust one another, they are more likely to be open and vulnerable with one another, which can help to foster empathy. Trust can also help to create a safe space for people to share their thoughts and feelings, which can help to foster empathy.

In summary, empathy and trust are mutually reinforcing, they build on each other, and they are both important aspects of effective communication and relationship building. Empathy can help to build trust, and trust can help to foster empathy. Salespeople and anyone else looking to build trust and foster empathy should focus on understanding and validating the feelings of others, and being responsive, reliable, and transparent. Additionally, they can also practice active listening, and open-ended questioning, and try to see things from the other person's point of view.

Empathy and Customer Needs

A salesperson needs the time to understand and acknowledge the customer's situation, rather than just trying to make a sale. This empathetic approach can help the salesperson to build trust and a deeper connection with the customer, which can ultimately lead to the outcome of a more successful sale.

Moreover, when salespeople can empathize with their customers, they can identify their pain points and tailor their offers to meet their needs. They can also anticipate their concerns and objections, and prepare effective responses. Also, empathy can help salespeople to create a sense of belonging and value for the customer, which can increase the chances of customer loyalty.

Additionally, empathy can also help salespeople to understand the customer's buying motivations and tailor their approach accordingly. For example, if a customer is motivated by cost savings, a salesperson can highlight how their product or service can help the customer save money.

In summary, empathy is a crucial aspect of understanding and meeting customer needs. By understanding and sharing the feelings of their customers, salespeople can better understand the customer's needs, concerns, and buying motivations, which can ultimately lead to more successful sales outcomes.

CHAPTER SIX

Critical Listening in Sales

Evaluating Customer Needs

Evaluating customer needs is an important step in the sales process, as it helps salespeople to understand what the customer is looking for and to tailor their approach accordingly. This can lead to more successful sales outcomes and can help to build trust and a deeper connection with the customer.

There are several ways that salespeople can evaluate customer needs, including:

Asking open-ended questions: Salespeople can ask open-ended questions to encourage the customer to share more information about their needs, concerns, and priorities. This can help the salesperson to understand the customer's perspective and to identify their pain points.

Active listening: Salespeople can use active listening skills to fully understand and absorb the information that the customer is sharing. This can help the salesperson to identify the customer's needs and to tailor their approach accordingly.

Observing body language: Salespeople can observe the customer's body language and nonverbal cues to gain insights into their needs and concerns. For example, if a customer is fidgeting or avoiding eye contact, this may indicate that they are uncomfortable or uncertain about something.

Analyzing customer data: Salespeople can use customer data, such as purchase history or demographic information, to gain insights into the customer's needs and preferences.

Using empathy: Salespeople can use empathy to understand and share the feelings of their customers, which can help them to identify their pain points and tailor their approach accordingly.

In summary, evaluating customer needs is an important step in the sales process, as it helps salespeople to understand what the customer is looking for and to tailor their approach accordingly. By using a combination of open-ended questions, active listening, observation, data analysis, and empathy, salespeople can gain a deeper understanding of their customers and offer solutions that meet their specific needs.

Open-ended questions and sales

Open-ended questions are a valuable tool for salespeople, as they allow them to gather more information about the customer's needs, concerns, and priorities. These types of questions are designed to encourage the customer to share more information and to provide the salesperson with a deeper understanding of the customer's perspective.

Examples of open-ended questions that salespeople can use include:

Can you tell me more about your current situation?

What are your main concerns or priorities in relation to this product/service?

How do you currently handle this problem?

What would you like to achieve with this product/service?

How can I help you to achieve your goals?

Using open-ended questions can help the salesperson to understand the customer's perspective, identify their pain points, and tailor their approach accordingly. It also allows the salesperson to understand the customer's needs and expectations and can help to build trust and a deeper connection with the customer.

Additionally, open-ended questions can also help to steer the conversation away from the features and benefits of the product or service, and instead focus on the customer's needs, goals and priorities. This can help the salesperson to understand the customer's needs and to offer solutions that meet those needs.

In summary, open-ended questions are an important tool for salespeople, as they allow them to gather more information about the customer's needs, concerns, and priorities. By using open-ended questions, salespeople can gain a deeper understanding of the customer's perspective, identify their pain points and tailor their approach accordingly, build trust, and offer solutions that meet the customer's specific needs.

Active listening and sales

Active listening is a key skill for salespeople, as it allows them to fully understand and absorb the information that the customer is sharing. Active listening involves paying close attention to what the customer is saying, both verbally and non-verbally, and providing verbal and non-verbal feedback to show that the salesperson is engaged and interested in what the customer has to say.

Examples of active listening techniques that salespeople can use include:

Rephrasing or paraphrasing what the customer has said to show that the salesperson has understood their message

Asking follow-up questions to gather more information and to clarify any points that are unclear

Providing nonverbal cues, such as nodding or making eye contact, to show that the salesperson is engaged and interested in what the customer has to say.

Active listening can help the salesperson to understand the customer's perspective, identify their pain points, and tailor their approach accordingly. It also allows the salesperson to understand the customer's needs and expectations, which can help to build trust and a deeper connection with the customer. Additionally, active listening can also help to steer the conversation away from the features and benefits of the product or service, and instead focus on the customer's needs, goals and priorities.

Active listening can also help the salesperson identify buying signals, this is the verbal and nonverbal cues that indicate that the customer is ready to buy. Identifying buying signals can help the salesperson to close the sale at the right time, and avoid pushing the customer too hard or too soon, which can lead to losing the sale.

In summary, Active listening is a key skill for salespeople, as it allows them to fully understand and absorb the information that the customer is sharing. It helps the salesperson to understand the customer's perspective, identify their pain points, tailor their approach accordingly, build trust and a deeper connection with the customer, and identify buying signals to close the sale.

Body language and sales

Body language is an important aspect of communication, and it can play a significant role in sales interactions. Salespeople can use body language to convey interest and engagement, build trust and rapport with the customer, and influence the customer's perception of the salesperson and the product or service being sold.

Examples of positive body language that salespeople can use include:

- Maintaining eye contact to show interest and engagement
- Smiling to convey a friendly and approachable demeanor

- Using an open and relaxed body posture to show that the salesperson is confident and trustworthy
- Leaning forward to showing interest and engagement
- Using gestures to emphasize points and convey enthusiasm

It's also important for salespeople to be aware of their own body language and to be mindful of the customer's body language during the interaction. Salespeople can observe the customer's body language for cues about their level of interest or engagement, such as crossed arms, which may indicate defensiveness or a lack of interest.

Additionally, salespeople should also be mindful of cultural differences in body language, as gestures and expressions that are considered positive in one culture may be considered negative in another culture.

In summary, body language is an important aspect of communication, and it can play a significant role in sales interactions. Salespeople can use body language to convey interest and engagement, build trust and rapport with the customer, and influence the customer's perception of the salesperson and the product or service being sold. It is also important for salespeople to be aware of their own body language and the customer's body language, and to be mindful of cultural differences in body language.

Customer data and sales

Using customer data can be a powerful tool for salespeople, as it allows them to better understand the customer's needs and preferences, and to tailor their sales pitch accordingly. Customer data can be collected through various means such as surveys, website analytics, customer interactions, and purchase history.

For example, a salesperson may use customer data to:

Identify the customer's pain points and tailor their sales pitch to address those specific concerns

Personalize the sales pitch by addressing the customer by name and referencing their previous interactions or purchases

Understand the customer's buying history and suggest complementary products or services

Identify patterns in customer behavior, such as when they are most likely to make a purchase, and time their sales pitch accordingly

Identify the customer's communication preferences, such as phone or email, and use that information to contact the customer in a way that is most likely to be well-received.

Using customer data can help salespeople to build stronger relationships with customers by showing that they understand and value the customer's needs and preferences. Additionally, it can also help salespeople to be more efficient and effective in their sales efforts by targeting their pitch to the most likely buyers.

However, it's important for salespeople to be aware of the ethical and legal implications of using customer data. Salespeople should ensure that they have obtained the customer's consent to use their data and that they are using the data only for the purpose for which it was collected. They should also ensure that they are complying with any relevant data privacy regulations, such as the General Data Protection Regulation (GDPR) in the EU or the California Consumer Privacy Act (CCPA) in the US.

In summary, using customer data can be a powerful tool for salespeople, as it allows them to better understand the customer's needs and preferences, and to tailor their sales pitch accordingly. Salespeople can use customer data to identify the customer's pain points, personalize the sales pitch, suggest complementary products or services, and identify patterns in customer behavior. However, it's important for salespeople to be aware of the ethical and legal implications of using customer data, and ensure that they have obtained the customer's consent to use their data and comply with relevant data privacy regulations.

Empathy and sales

Empathy is the ability to understand and share the feelings of another person, and it can be a valuable asset for salespeople in building and maintaining relationships with customers. Empathy can help salespeople to understand the customer's perspective, build trust and rapport, and tailor their sales pitch to the customer's specific needs and concerns.

For example, a salesperson who demonstrates empathy by actively listening to a customer's concerns and validating their feelings is more likely to build a strong relationship with the customer. This can lead to the customer feeling more comfortable and open to buying from the salesperson. Additionally, an empathetic salesperson can also anticipate the customer's needs and concerns and be better prepared to address them.

Empathy can also help salespeople to build stronger relationships with their customers by showing that they understand and value their needs and concerns. Additionally, empathetic salespeople can also be more efficient and effective in their sales efforts by identifying and addressing the customer's pain points, building trust and rapport, and tailoring their sales pitch to the customer's specific needs and preferences.

However, it's important to note that empathy can be difficult to demonstrate in virtual or remote sales interactions. It is harder to read body language and tone of voice and it is more challenging to build trust and rapport with the customer. In these cases, salespeople may need to use other techniques to demonstrate empathy, such as active listening, showing empathy through their words, and asking open-ended questions.

In summary, Empathy is the ability to understand and share the feelings of another person, it is valuable for salespeople to build and maintain relationships with customers. Empathy can help salespeople understand the customer's perspective, build trust and rapport, and tailor their sales pitch to the customer's specific needs and concerns. It is also important for salespeople to be aware of the challenges of demonstrating empathy in virtual or remote interactions, and to use other techniques such as active listening, showing empathy through words, and asking open-ended questions to build trust and rapport with the customer.

Distinguishing facts from opinions

Distinguishing facts from opinions is an important skill for salespeople, as it allows them to communicate information accurately and effectively. Facts are statements that can be proven to be true or false, while opinions are statements that reflect a personal viewpoint or belief.

For example, a fact would be "This product has a 5-year warranty," while an opinion would be "This product is the best on the market."

When communicating with customers, it's important for salespeople to distinguish between facts and opinions. This helps to establish trust and credibility with customers, as they can be assured that the information they are receiving is accurate. It also helps salespeople to avoid making claims that cannot be supported by evidence, which can damage their credibility and the customer's trust.

Additionally, distinguishing facts from opinions can also help salespeople to address any objections or concerns that the customer may have. For example, if a customer expresses a concern about a product's durability, a salesperson can provide facts about the product's warranty or testing results to address the concern, rather than providing an opinion about the product's durability.

In summary, distinguishing facts from opinions is an important skill for salespeople, as it allows them to communicate information accurately and effectively. This helps to establish trust and credibility with customers, as they can be assured that the information they are receiving is accurate. It also helps salespeople to avoid making claims that cannot be supported by evidence, which can damage their credibility and the customer's trust. Additionally, distinguishing facts from opinions can also help salespeople to address any objections or concerns that the customer may have.

Distinguish facts from propaganda

Distinguishing facts from propaganda is an important skill for salespeople, as it allows them to communicate information accurately and effectively to their customers. Salespeople must be able to provide their customers with accurate and unbiased information about their products or services in order to build trust and credibility.

One way for salespeople to distinguish facts from propaganda is to be familiar with their products or services and the industry they are working in. This allows them to identify any false or misleading claims made by competitors and to present accurate information to their customers.

Another way is to be able to provide evidence to support the claims they make about their products or services. For example, if a salesperson claims that a product has a certain feature, they should be able to provide documentation or other evidence to support this claim. Salespeople should also be able to provide references or testimonials from satisfied customers, which can serve as independent validation of the claims they make.

Salespeople should also be aware of the use of emotional appeals or sensationalism in the marketing materials of their competitors, and avoid using these tactics themselves. They should instead focus on providing accurate and objective information about the benefits and features of their products or services.

Additionally, in order to protect both the company and themselves from liability, salespeople should be aware of any regulations or laws that may apply to their industry and ensure that they are not making any claims that could be considered false or misleading.

In summary, distinguishing facts from propaganda is an important skill for salespeople, as it allows them to communicate information accurately and effectively to their customers. Salespeople should be familiar with their products or services and the industry they are working in, be able to provide evidence to support the claims they make, avoid using emotional appeals or sensationalism, and be aware of any regulations or laws that may apply to their industry. This will help them build trust and credibility with their customers, and ensure that they and the company are not engaging in any illegal or unethical practices.

CHAPTER SEVEN

Listening in Different Sales Contexts

Listening is a critical skill for salespeople, but the nuances of listening can vary depending on the sales setting. Here are a few examples of how the nuances of listening can vary in different sales settings:

In-person sales: In an in-person sales setting, the salesperson can use nonverbal cues such as body language, facial expressions, and tone of voice to indicate that they are actively listening to the customer. Additionally, the salesperson can use open-ended questions to encourage the customer to share more information and build a deeper understanding of their needs.

Phone sales: In a phone sales setting, the salesperson needs to rely more heavily on verbal cues such as active listening, reflecting, and summarizing to show the customer that they are actively listening. Additionally, the salesperson should pay attention to the customer's tone of voice, which can indicate their level of engagement or interest.

Online sales: In an online sales setting, the salesperson needs to rely on written communication to indicate that they are actively listening to the customer. This can be done by providing detailed responses to customer inquiries and asking follow-up questions to gain a deeper understanding of their needs.

Virtual sales: Virtual sales can be similar to online sales, but with the added layer of video communication. In this setting, the salesperson must pay attention to both verbal and nonverbal cues, just like in in-person sales. Additionally, the salesperson should ensure that the virtual environment is set up for optimal communication, such as good lighting and audio quality.

Cross-cultural sales: In cross-cultural sales, the nuances of listening can vary greatly depending on the cultural background of the customer. Salespeople should be aware of cultural differences in communication styles, such as the use of indirect language or the importance of nonverbal cues, and adjust their listening styles accordingly.

It's important to be aware of the nuances of listening in different sales settings and to adapt your listening style accordingly. This can help to build trust and credibility with your customers and ultimately lead to more successful sales.

In-person sales and listening

In-person sales settings provide the opportunity for salespeople to use a variety of listening skills and techniques to actively engage with customers and build trust.

One of the key listening skills in an in-person sales setting is active listening. This involves paying full attention to the customer, making eye contact, nodding, and providing verbal cues such as "I understand" or "I see" to show that the salesperson is fully engaged in the conversation.

Another important technique is the use of open-ended questions. By asking open-ended questions, salespeople can encourage customers to share more information about their needs and wants, which can help the salesperson to better understand the customer's perspective and tailor their sales pitch accordingly.

In addition to active listening and open-ended questions, salespeople should also be aware of nonverbal cues such as body language and facial expressions. For example, a customer who is crossing their arms or avoiding eye contact may be indicating that they are not fully engaged or that they are not interested in what the salesperson has to say. Salespeople should be able to read these cues and adjust their approach accordingly.

It's also important for salespeople to be aware of their own body language, as this can also have an impact on the customer's perception of them. Salespeople should maintain good eye contact, keep an open and relaxed posture, and avoid fidgeting or other distracting behaviors.

An in-person sales setting also provides an opportunity for salespeople to build trust with their customers by empathizing with their needs and wants. By putting themselves in the customer's shoes, salespeople can better understand their perspective and provide solutions that align with their needs.

In summary, in-person sales settings provide a unique opportunity for salespeople to use a variety of listening skills and techniques to actively engage with customers and build trust. These include active listening, open-ended questions, being aware of nonverbal cues, maintaining good body language, and building trust through empathy.

Phone sales and listening

Phone sales settings present some unique challenges for salespeople when it comes to listening effectively. Because they cannot rely on nonverbal cues such as body language and facial expressions, salespeople must rely more heavily on verbal cues to indicate that they are actively listening to the customer.

One of the key listening skills in a phone sales setting is active listening. This involves paying full attention to the customer, avoiding interrupting, and providing verbal cues such as "I understand" or "I see" to show that the salesperson is fully engaged in the conversation.

Another important technique is the use of reflective listening. This involves repeating or paraphrasing what the customer has said to show that the salesperson has understood their message and to ensure that there is no misunderstanding. Reflective listening can help to build trust and credibility with the customer, as it shows that the salesperson is fully engaged and attentive.

In addition, summarizing what the customer has said at the end of a conversation or a key point of it can help to ensure that both parties are on the same page and provide an opportunity for the customer to correct any misunderstandings.

It's also important for salespeople to be aware of the customer's tone of voice, which can indicate their level of engagement or interest. A customer who is speaking in a monotone voice or using filler words such as "um" or "ah" may be indicating that they are not fully engaged or that they are not interested in what the salesperson has to say.

In phone sales, it can be more difficult to build trust and rapport with the customer as compared to in-person sales. However, by using active listening, reflective listening, and summarizing, salespeople can still demonstrate that they are fully engaged and attentive and build trust with the customer over the phone.

In summary, Phone sales settings present some unique challenges for salespeople when it comes to listening effectively, but by using active listening, reflective listening, summarizing, and being aware of the customer's tone of voice, salespeople can still effectively build trust and engage with customers over the phone.

Online sales and listening

Online sales settings present a different set of challenges when it comes to listening effectively as compared to in-person and phone sales.

One of the key listening skills in an online sales setting is active reading. This involves paying full attention to the customer's message, avoiding interrupting, and providing verbal or written cues such as "I understand" or "I see" to show that the salesperson is fully engaged in the conversation.

Another important technique is the use of reflective listening. This can be done by paraphrasing or summarizing what the customer has said to show that the salesperson has understood their message and to ensure that there is no misunderstanding. Reflective listening can help to build trust and credibility with the customer, as it shows that the salesperson is fully engaged and attentive.

In online sales, it's also important for the salesperson to be aware of the customer's tone and choice of words in their message. This can indicate their level of engagement or interest. A customer who is using negative or dismissive language may be indicating that they are not fully engaged or that they are not interested in what the salesperson has to say.

Building trust and rapport with the customer can be more difficult in online sales as compared to in-person and phone sales, due to the lack of face-to-face interaction. However, by using active reading, reflective listening, and being aware of the customer's tone and choice of words, salespeople can still effectively engage with and build trust with customers in an online sales setting.

In summary, Online sales setting present a different set of challenges for salespeople when it comes to listening effectively as compared to in-person and phone sales. By using active reading, reflective listening, and being aware of the customer's tone and choice of words, salespeople can still effectively engage with and build trust with customers in an online sales setting.

Virtual sales and listening

Virtual sales settings refer to online sales that take place through video conferencing, such as Zoom or Webex. These settings present a unique combination of challenges and opportunities when it comes to listening effectively as compared to in-person, phone, and text-based online sales.

One of the key listening skills in a virtual sales setting is active listening. This involves paying full attention to the customer, avoiding interrupting, and providing verbal cues such as "I understand" or "I see" to show that the salesperson is fully engaged in the conversation. It's important to maintain eye contact, use open and relaxed body language, and smile when appropriate, which can help to build trust and rapport.

Another important technique is the use of reflective listening. This involves repeating or paraphrasing what the customer has said to show that the salesperson has understood their message and to ensure that there is no misunderstanding. Reflective listening can help to build trust and credibility with the customer, as it shows that the salesperson is fully engaged and attentive.

In virtual sales, it is important to be aware of the customer's nonverbal cues, such as their facial expressions and body language, which can indicate their level of engagement or interest. A customer who is looking away from the screen or has neutral or closed-off body language may be indicating that they are not fully engaged or that they are not interested in what the salesperson has to say.

Virtual sales settings provide the opportunity for the salesperson to build trust and rapport with the customer through face-to-face interaction, which can be more difficult in text-based online sales. However, by using active listening, reflective listening, being aware of the customer's nonverbal cues, and maintaining good eye contact and body language, salespeople can effectively engage with and build trust with customers in a virtual sales setting.

In summary, Virtual sales settings refer to online sales that take place through video conferencing and present a unique combination of challenges and opportunities when it comes to listening effectively as compared to in-person, phone, and text-based online sales. By using active listening, reflective listening, being aware of the customer's nonverbal cues and maintaining good eye contact and body language, salespeople can effectively engage with and build trust with customers in a virtual sales setting.

Cross-cultural sales and listening

Cross-cultural sales refer to situations where a salesperson is working with customers from different cultural backgrounds. In these situations, listening skills become even more important as cultural differences can affect communication styles and expectations.

One important aspect of cross-cultural sales is understanding the different communication styles of different cultures. For example, some cultures value indirect communication, where the message is conveyed through subtle hints and nonverbal cues, while others prefer direct communication, where the message is stated clearly and directly. Understanding these communication styles can help a salesperson listen more effectively and avoid misunderstandings.

Another important aspect of cross-cultural sales is being aware of cultural norms and expectations. For example, in some cultures, it is considered impolite to directly disagree with someone, while in others it is expected. Understanding these norms can help a salesperson listen more effectively and to respond in a way that is appropriate and respectful.

One technique that can be used in cross-cultural sales is reflective listening, which involves repeating or paraphrasing what the customer has said to show that the salesperson has understood their message. Reflective listening can be particularly useful in cross-cultural sales as it can help to build trust and credibility with the customer, as it shows that the salesperson is fully engaged and attentive.

Another technique that can be used in cross-cultural sales is active listening, which involves paying full attention to the customer, avoiding interrupting, and providing verbal cues such as "I understand" or "I see" to show that the salesperson is fully engaged in the conversation. Active listening can help to build trust and rapport with customers from different cultural backgrounds.

In summary, cross-cultural sales refers to situations where a salesperson is working with customers from different cultural backgrounds, and it is important to understand the different communication styles of different cultures and be aware of cultural norms and expectations. Techniques such as reflective listening and active listening can help to build trust and rapport with customers from different cultural backgrounds.

CHAPTER EIGHT

Improving Listening Skills for Sales

Strategies for developing and maintaining listening skills in sales

There are several strategies that salespeople can use to develop and maintain their listening skills:

- Practice active listening: One of the most effective ways to develop listening skills is to practice active listening in everyday conversations. This involves paying full attention to the speaker, avoiding interruptions, and providing verbal cues such as "I understand" or "I see" to show that you are fully engaged in the conversation.
- Seek feedback: It can be helpful to seek feedback from others on your listening skills. This can be done by asking colleagues, supervisors, or customers for their honest opinion on how well you listen and what areas you could improve.
- Reflect on your listening: Take the time to reflect on your listening habits and try to identify any patterns or areas that need improvement. This can be done through self-reflection, journaling, or working with a coach.
- Take a course or workshop: Another effective way to develop listening skills is to take a course or workshop specifically designed to improve listening skills. These programs typically include activities and exercises that help participants develop their listening skills in a structured and supportive environment.
- Keep learning: Keep learning about the different types of listening and how to apply them in different situations. This can be done through reading books, and articles, and attending webinars or seminars.
- Use technology: There are many mobile apps and online tools that can help improve listening skills, such as language learning apps, podcasts,

and online courses.

- Role-play: Role-playing different sales scenarios with a colleague or coach can help to build listening skills by simulating real-world situations and allowing you to practice your listening skills in a safe and supportive environment.
- Incorporate listening into your daily routine: make listening to a daily habit, by setting aside time each day to practice your listening skills and make them a regular part of your daily routine. This can be done by setting aside time to listen to podcasts, audiobooks, or other audio-based learning materials.
- Listen to understand, not to respond: In sales, it's important to understand the customer's needs, concerns and motivations. Listen to understand their perspective before responding.
- Show that you're listening: Provide verbal and nonverbal cues to indicate that you're paying attention, such as nodding your head, making eye contact, and using phrases like "I understand" or "I hear you."
- Keep an open mind: Be open to different perspectives and avoid jumping to conclusions. Keep an open mind and be willing to consider different points of view.
- Practice, practice, practice: Like any skill, listening requires practice. Make a commitment to actively work on your listening skills and be patient with yourself as you improve.

Developing listening skills is a continuous process that requires commitment and practice. Here are a few more tips on how to maintain and improve your listening skills:

Be present: When in a conversation, be fully present and avoid distractions such as checking your phone or thinking about other things.

Listen with your whole body: In addition to using your ears to listen, also use your body language to indicate that you're paying attention. This can include maintaining eye contact, nodding, and using open and relaxed body language.

Listen for the main idea: When listening, focus on the main idea or message being conveyed, rather than getting caught up in the details.

Listen for emotions: Pay attention to the emotions being expressed by the speaker, as these can provide valuable insight into their perspective and needs.

Be patient: Listening takes time and patience. Avoid interrupting or rushing the speaker, and give them the time they need to fully express themselves.

Listen for what isn't said: Be aware of nonverbal cues, such as tone of voice, facial expressions, and body language, as these can convey important information that isn't being said directly.

Reflect and adapt: After each conversation, reflect on your listening skills and think about what worked well and what could be improved. Then, make adjustments and adapt your listening style as needed.

Practice in different settings: Practice listening in different settings, such as in person, over the phone, and online. This will help you to develop the flexibility and adaptability needed to be a successful listener in any situation.

Seek out diverse perspectives: Listen to people with different backgrounds, cultures, and experiences. This will help you to develop empathy and understanding, as well as to expand your perspective and improve your listening skills.

Seek out diverse perspectives: Listen to people with different backgrounds, cultures, and experiences. This will help you to develop empathy and understanding, as well as to expand your perspective and improve your listening skills.

Listen to feedback: Listen to feedback from your customers, colleagues, and supervisor. This will help you to understand how well you are listening and what areas you need to improve.

Take responsibility for your listening: Remember that listening is a skill that you can develop and improve and that it is ultimately your responsibility to do so.

CHAPTER NINE

Case Studies

Examples of listening skills in action in real-world sales scenarios

Example 1

Here's an example of listening skills in action in a real-world sales scenario:

A salesperson is working with a customer who is looking to purchase a new car. The customer expresses that they are concerned about the car's fuel efficiency and how it will fit into their budget. The salesperson actively listens to the customer's concerns and asks open-ended questions to better understand their needs. They also pay attention to nonverbal cues, such as the customer's body language, to get a sense of their level of interest and concern.

The salesperson then provides the customer with information on the fuel efficiency of the car and how it compares to other models in its class. They also provide information on financing options and how the customer can make the car fit into their budget. Throughout the conversation, the salesperson maintains a calm and supportive tone of voice and uses empathetic listening to validate the customer's concerns.

As a result, the customer feels heard and understood, which helps to build trust and rapport with the salesperson. The customer ultimately makes a purchase, feeling confident that the car is the right fit for them and their budget.

It's important to note that the example above is just a general one and that each customer is unique and should be treated differently, but the key here is that the salesperson is using active listening to understand the customer's needs, using empathy and showing concern and understanding, and providing the right information that would help the customer make a decision.

Example 2

Here's another example of listening skills in action in a real-world sales scenario:

A salesperson is working with a customer who is looking to purchase new software for their business. The customer expresses that they are concerned about the cost of the software and how it will integrate with their current systems. The salesperson actively listens to the customer's concerns, asking open-ended questions to better understand their needs and pain points, and also makes sure to note key information about the customer's business, such as current systems in use and the size of their company.

The salesperson then provides the customer with a detailed breakdown of the software's costs, including any potential savings they could see from using it, as well as a demonstration of how the software would integrate with their current systems. The salesperson also makes sure to go over the features of the software that would be of most benefit to the customer, based on the information he gathered about their business.

Throughout the conversation, the salesperson maintains a calm and professional tone of voice and uses empathetic listening to validate the customer's concerns.

As a result, the customer feels heard and understood, which helps to build trust and rapport with the salesperson, and they ultimately make the purchase, feeling confident that the software is the right fit for their business and their budget.

Again, it's worth noting that this is just one example and that each customer is unique and should be treated differently, but the key here is that the salesperson is using active listening to understand the customer's needs, gathering information about their business, and providing the right information that would help the customer make a decision.

Example 3

Here's another example of listening skills in action in a real-world sales scenario:

A salesperson is working with a customer who is looking to purchase a new software for their business. The customer expresses that they are concerned about the software's compatibility with their current systems, as well as its ability to integrate with other systems they plan to use in the future.

The salesperson actively listens to the customer's concerns and asks open-ended questions to better understand their needs. They also take notes on the customer's specific requirements and concerns to ensure that they are providing accurate and relevant information.

The salesperson then provides the customer with detailed information about the software's compatibility and integration capabilities, as well as any potential challenges that might arise. They also provide information on any additional support or services that can help the customer with the integration process.

Throughout the conversation, the salesperson demonstrates a deep understanding of the customer's concerns and provides solutions that address those concerns. The customer feels that the salesperson has truly listened to them and understands their needs, and ultimately decides to purchase the software.

It's important to note that the example above is just a general one and that each customer is unique and should be treated differently, but the key here is that the salesperson is using active listening to understand the customer's needs, using empathy and showing concern and understanding, and providing the right information that would help the customer make a decision.

Example 4

Here's another example of listening skills in action in a real-world sales scenario:

A salesperson is working with a customer who is looking to purchase a new service. The customer expresses that they are hesitant to commit to the service due to a previous bad experience with a similar service provider. The salesperson actively listens to the customer's concerns and empathizes with their experience. They validate the customer's feelings and acknowledge the importance of their trust.

The salesperson then provides the customer with detailed information about the service, highlighting the ways in which it is different from the previous service the customer used. They also provide information about the company's history, reputation, and customer satisfaction rate. The salesperson also offers to provide references and testimonials from satisfied customers.

Throughout the conversation, the salesperson demonstrates a deep understanding of the customer's concerns and provides solutions that address those concerns. The customer feels that the salesperson has truly listened to them and understands their needs, and ultimately decides to purchase the service.

It's important to note that the example above is just a general one and that each customer is unique and should be treated differently, but the key here is that the salesperson is using active listening to understand the customer's needs, using empathy and showing concern and understanding, and providing the right information that would help the customer make a decision.

Example 5

Here's another example of listening skills in action in a real-world sales scenario:

A salesperson is working with a customer who is looking to purchase a new product but is unsure of which option to choose. The salesperson actively listens to the customer's needs and concerns and asks questions to better understand their priorities. They also pay attention to the customer's nonverbal cues, such as body language and tone of voice, to gain additional insight into their decision-making process.

The salesperson then provides the customer with detailed information about each of the options available, highlighting the pros and cons of each. They also provide examples of how other customers have used the product successfully in similar scenarios.

Throughout the conversation, the salesperson demonstrates a deep understanding of the customer's needs and helps the customer make an informed decision. The customer feels that the salesperson has truly listened to them and that their needs have been taken into account.

It's important to note that the example above is just a general one and that each customer is unique and should be treated differently, but the key here is that the salesperson is using active listening to understand the customer's needs, using empathy and showing concern and understanding, and providing the right information that would help the customer make a decision.

Conclusion

Here are some key points to remember when it comes to listening in sales:

Active listening: This involves truly paying attention to what the customer is saying, both verbally and nonverbally. This helps salespeople to better understand the customer's needs and concerns.

Empathy: By putting themselves in the customer's shoes, salespeople can better understand their perspective and provide solutions that address their specific needs.

Reflective listening: This involves restating or paraphrasing what the customer has said, to ensure that the salesperson has accurately understood their concerns.

Summarizing: This involves briefly summarizing the main points of the conversation, to ensure that both the customer and the salesperson are on the same page.

Avoiding assumptions and interruptions: Salespeople should avoid making assumptions about the customer's needs and should avoid interrupting the customer while they are speaking.

Maintaining eye contact and open body language: This shows the customer that the salesperson is engaged and interested in what they have to say.

Being honest and transparent: A salesperson should be honest and transparent with their customer and should not make false promises or claims.

Maintaining a calm and supportive tone of voice: This can help to put the customer at ease and build trust.

Being adaptable to different cultures and languages: Salespeople should be mindful of cultural and language differences when communicating with customers from diverse backgrounds.

Continual self-improvement: Listening skills are something that can be practiced and developed over time, so salespeople should continually work on improving their listening skills.

In summary, effective listening skills are crucial for salespeople. They help salespeople to better understand the customer, build trust, and provide solutions that address the customer's specific needs, which ultimately leads to more successful sales.

Additional resources for further learning

There are many resources available for those looking to further develop their listening skills in the context of sales. Here are a few examples:

Books: There are a number of books on the topic of listening skills in sales, such as "The Art of Active Listening" by Jim Cathcart, "The Lost Art of Listening" by Michael Nichols, and "Crucial Conversations: Tools for Talking When Stakes Are High" by Kerry Patterson.

Courses: Online courses and webinars on the topic of listening skills in sales are widely available, such as "Active Listening for Sales Professionals" and "Empathetic Listening in Sales".

Sales training programs: Many sales training programs include modules on listening skills, such as "The Challenger Sale" and "SPIN Selling." I also offer a training program on "Listening Skills".

Professional development workshops: Many companies offer workshops and training programs on listening skills for sales professionals as part of their employee development offerings.

Podcasts: There are many podcasts that focus on sales and business, such as "The Sales Evangelist" and "The Salesman Podcast" that offer tips and strategies for developing listening skills.

Coaching: Some salespeople may benefit from working one-on-one with a coach or mentor who can provide personalized feedback and guidance on their listening skills.

Practice: The best way to develop listening skills is to practice, practice and practice. Salespeople should actively seek out opportunities to listen to customers, take notes and reflect on their own listening skills.

In addition to these resources, it's important to remember that listening is a skill that can be continuously developed and improved over time, so it's important to be patient and persistent in your efforts to improve.

Appendix

Exercises

There are several exercises that can be used to practice active listening, which can help salespeople develop the skills they need to effectively engage with customers and build trust. Here are a few examples:

Listening partner exercise: Find a partner and take turns having a conversation while the other person actively listens. After each conversation, the listener should summarize what they heard and provide feedback on how well they felt they listened.

Role-playing: Salespeople can practice active listening in a simulated sales situation by role-playing a conversation with a customer. This can be done with a colleague or a coach, who can provide feedback on how well the salesperson is listening.

Mirroring: During a conversation, repeat back to the speaker what you've heard them say in your own words. This can help you to better understand their perspective and demonstrate that you are actively listening.

Asking open-ended questions: Instead of simply responding to what a customer says, ask open-ended questions that encourage them to share more information.

Reflecting feelings: When the customer expresses a feeling, take the time to reflect on it, using phrases like "It sounds like you're feeling...", "I can tell that this is important to you because...". This way you are showing that you are paying attention and that you understand their feelings.

Listen to your customer in silence: Sometimes the best way to listen is to just be quiet and let the customer speak without interruption. This can help you to better understand their perspective and identify key points that can be used to tailor your sales approach.

Track your progress: Keep a log of your listening activities, noting areas where you struggled and areas where you felt you were successful. Reflect on this log regularly to identify patterns and areas for improvement.

Practicing these exercises can help salespeople develop the listening skills they need to effectively engage with customers and build trust. It's important to remember that active listening is a skill that requires practice, patience, and persistence.

Worksheets

There are several worksheets that can be used to practice active listening, which can help salespeople develop the skills they need to effectively engage with customers and build trust. Here are a few examples:

Active Listening Checklist: This worksheet provides a list of key active listening skills, such as maintaining eye contact, avoiding interrupting, and summarizing, that salespeople can use to evaluate their own listening performance.

Reflective Listening Worksheet: This worksheet encourages salespeople to reflect on their listening skills by asking them to write down a conversation they had with a customer, identify areas where they could have listened more effectively, and note what they will do differently next time.

Empathetic Listening Worksheet: This worksheet encourages salespeople to put themselves in their customers' shoes by asking them to imagine how a customer might be feeling and then write down how they would respond in a way that shows empathy.

Active Listening Scenarios: This worksheet provides a series of scenarios that salespeople can use to practice active listening. For each scenario, salespeople are prompted to consider how they would respond and then reflect on how well they think they listened.

Listening Self-Assessment: This worksheet encourages salespeople to reflect on their own listening skills by asking them a series of questions about how they typically listen and what they could do to improve.

Listening and Summarizing: This worksheet encourages salespeople to practice active listening by having them listen to a short audio clip, take notes and then summarize the key points discussed.

Listening and Questioning: This worksheet encourages salespeople to practice asking an open-ended questions, based on the customer's statement, in order to gather more information.

These worksheets can be used as a guide to practice and improve active listening skills. It can be especially beneficial to use them in conjunction with regular training, coaching or self-reflection.

References And Bibliography

Here are a few references that could be included in a book about listening skills for salespeople:

"Crucial Conversations: Tools for Talking When Stakes Are High" by Kerry Patterson, Joseph Grenny, Ron McMillan, and Al Switzler. This book provides practical tools for improving communication and building stronger relationships, which are essential for effective listening in sales.

"Active Listening: Improve Your Ability to Listen and Lead" by Chris Croft. This book provides practical advice and exercises for developing active listening skills, including tips for building rapport, understanding body language, and handling difficult conversations.

"Nonviolent Communication: A Language of Life" by Marshall Rosenberg. This book provides a framework for understanding and practicing empathetic listening, which is essential for building trust and understanding customer needs in sales.

"Difficult Conversations: How to Discuss What Matters Most" by Douglas Stone, Bruce Patton, and Sheila Heen. This book provides strategies for handling difficult conversations in a way that builds understanding and maintains relationships, which is important in sales.

"Selling with Emotional Intelligence" by Colleen Stanley. This book provides insights and strategies for using emotional intelligence to build stronger relationships and close more sales, emphasizing the importance of empathy and active listening.

"The Lost Art of Listening: How Learning to Listen Can Improve Relationships" by Michael P. Nichols. This book provides an in-depth look at the importance of listening in building and maintaining relationships and includes practical strategies for improving listening skills.

"The Influence of Language on Culture and Thought: An Exploration of Linguistic Relativity" by Joshua Fishman. This book provides an overview of the impact of language on communication and understanding, which can be important in cross-cultural sales.

"The Art of Communicating" by Thich Nhat Hanh. This book provides insights and techniques for practicing mindful communication, which can be important for building trust and understanding in sales.

These references can be used as a guide to further research and understanding on listening skills in sales. It can be especially beneficial to use them in conjunction with the content of your book.